The B2B Sales Presentation

A presentation is not just an exposition of information; it is an opportunity to connect, persuade, and build trust. More than a simple speech, a successful presentation becomes an art form that allows you to weave a compelling narrative, master body language and emotions, and create a memorable experience that drives action.

The B2B Sales Presentation

Legal Information

Book Title: The B2B Sales Presentation

Copyright: All rights reserved. Reproduction of this book in e-Book or print version is strictly prohibited without the express written consent of the author, including partial or complete reproduction in any form or manner.

Author: Dionisio Melo

Publisher: Independent Publication

Year: 2024

ISBN: 9798332437298

The B2B Sales Presentation

Contents

Introduction Page 6

Chapter 1 Page 8
Laying the Groundwork: Keys to a Presentation

Chapter 2 Page 10
Knowing Your Audience

Chapter 3 Page 12
The "Why" Behind Your Presentation: A Clear Objective for Convincing Success

Chapter 4 Page 15
Structure and Content: Guiding Your Audience to Capture Their Attention

Chapter 5 Page 18
Concise and Persuasive Body

Chapter 6 Page 20
Impactful Conclusion
Leaving a Lasting Impression on Your Audience's Mind

The B2B Sales Presentation

Chapter 7 Page 22
Mastering the Stage
Tips for a Successful Presentation
Body Language and Non-Verbal
Communication: Beyond Words

Chapter 8 Page 25
Effective Communication
Speaking with Passion and Enthusiasm,
Connecting with Your Audience

Chapter 9 Page 27
Mastering the Tools
Visual Resources that Capture Attention
and Clarify the Message

Chapter 10 Page 30
Time Management
A Precious Resource to Respect

Chapter 11 Page 32
Tips to Capture Attention and Generate
Interest
Connecting with Emotions Through
Stories and Examples

The B2B Sales Presentation

Chapter 12 Page 34
Incorporate Humor
A Touch of Lightness for a Memorable Presentation

Chapter 13 Page 37
Create Interaction
Engage Your Audience and Foster Conversation

Epilogue Page 39

About the Author Page 40

The B2B Sales Presentation

Introduction

In today's B2B sales landscape, where information flows rapidly and decision-making is based on logic and thoroughness, an effective presentation has become a critical success factor. It's no longer just about showcasing a product or service but about creating a memorable experience that captivates the audience, generates interest, and drives them to take action. More than just a speech, a successful B2B presentation is an art cultivated through practice and perfected with experience.

This book will equip you with the tools for B2B sales presentations, strategies, and techniques that will enable you to capture attention, persuade your audience, and become a true master of commercial communication.

Meticulous preparation, mastering body language, simple language, and the strategic use of visual aids can transform an ordinary

The B2B Sales Presentation

presentation into an experience that propels you toward closing a successful deal.

Discover how to build a compelling narrative that connects with the needs and aspirations of your potential clients, how to use body language to convey confidence and credibility, and how to leverage digital tools to create an interactive experience that leaves a lasting impression.

You will learn to become a persuasive speaker who inspires action, master the art of persuasion, and turn your presentations into a growth engine for your business.

Get ready to delve into the world of B2B sales presentations, where words, images, and emotions combine to create a transformative experience.

Prepare to learn, be inspired, and become a master of persuasion in the business realm.

Chapter 1
Laying the Groundwork: Keys to an Impactful Presentation

The secret to a successful B2B presentation lies in a deep understanding of your audience. More than just a speech, an effective presentation becomes a personalized conversation, a response to the needs and aspirations of your target audience. To build this crucial connection, it is essential to invest time in thoroughly researching who you are addressing.

Investigate their industry, needs, challenges, and pain points. What problems are they looking to solve? What value do they seek in a product or service? What are their main motivations? What type of language do they use? What information is relevant to them?

Answering these questions will allow you to create a presentation that resonates with your audience, connects with their needs, and offers a solution to their problems.

The B2B Sales Presentation

Remember, a presentation is not a monologue but an opportunity to initiate a dialogue that generates trust and conviction.

Imagine for a moment: Would you like to listen to a presentation that disregards your needs, doesn't relate to your challenges, or uses language that feels foreign to you? The answer is clear: No one wants to feel their time and attention are wasted.

Meticulous preparation and a deep understanding of your audience will enable you to create a presentation that is relevant, engaging, and persuasive.

This preparation allows you to become a reliable interlocutor who offers real solutions to the problems your audience faces. Remember, the key to building a successful presentation lies in connecting with your audience on a profound level, understanding their needs, and offering them a solution that meets their expectations

Chapter 2
Knowing Your Audience

The key to success lies in understanding who you are addressing. Research their industry, needs, challenges, and pain points. What problems are they looking to solve? What value do they seek in a product or service? What are their main motivations? What type of language do they use? What information is relevant to them?

Answering these questions will enable you to create a presentation that resonates with your audience, connects with their needs, and offers a solution to their problems.

Remember, a presentation is not a monologue but an opportunity to initiate a dialogue that generates trust and conviction.

Imagine for a moment: Would you like to listen to a presentation that disregards your needs, doesn't relate to your challenges, or uses language that feels foreign to you? The

The B2B Sales Presentation

answer is clear: No one wants to feel their time and attention are wasted.

Meticulous preparation and a deep understanding of your audience will enable you to create a presentation that is relevant, engaging, and persuasive. This preparation will help you become a reliable interlocutor who offers real solutions to the problems your audience faces.

The key to building a successful presentation lies in connecting with your audience on a profound level, understanding their needs, and offering them a solution that meets their expectations.

Chapter 3
The "Why" Behind Your Presentation: A Clear Objective for Convincing Success

A successful presentation doesn't arise from improvisation but from a well-defined strategy nourished by a clear and specific objective.

Before diving into constructing visuals and crafting arguments for your presentation, it is essential to reflect on the "why" behind it. What do you want to achieve with it?

Precisely define the goal of your presentation. Do you want to secure a business deal? Generate leads for future business opportunities? Inform about a new product or service? Present an innovative solution to a specific problem?

A clear objective will serve as your compass, guiding your message and orienting your strategy. It will allow you to

The B2B Sales Presentation

focus your content, select the most appropriate tools, and design a compelling call to action.

Imagine for a moment: What would happen if you tried to build a house without a blueprint? The result would likely be chaotic and dysfunctional. Similarly, a presentation without a defined objective will feel disconnected, scattered, and unconvincing.

A clear objective allows you to achieve three things:

Focus Your Message: It helps you prioritize relevant information and eliminate elements that do not align with your purpose.

Select the Right Tools: It enables you to choose the visual and narrative tools that best suit your objective.

Design an Effective Call to Action: It guides your audience towards the desired action, whether it's scheduling a meeting,

The B2B Sales Presentation

downloading informational material, or making a purchase.

A presentation with a defined objective is like a ship with a clear course, sailing towards success with purpose and a well-defined strategy.

Chapter 4
Structure and Content: Guiding Your Audience to Capture Their Attention

Once you have defined the objective of your presentation and understand your audience, it's time to shape the structure and content that will make it engaging, informative, and persuasive.

Imagine your presentation as a journey, a voyage that takes your audience from point A to point B, guiding them through information and turning them into ambassadors of your message.

To achieve this goal, it is essential to structure your presentation logically and attractively, using a sequence that keeps the audience engaged and intrigued every step of the way.

A Strong Start is crucial to capturing attention from the outset. The beginning of

The B2B Sales Presentation

your presentation is pivotal—it's the first impression you'll make on your audience and will determine whether they remain interested or disconnect. To avoid disengagement, it's essential to capture attention right from the start with a compelling introduction that sparks curiosity and interest.

How do you achieve a compelling introduction? Here are some ideas:

A Provocative Question: Pose a question that engages the audience and prompts them to reflect on the topic you're about to address.

An Impactful Statistic: Share a relevant statistic that demonstrates the importance of the topic and grabs the audience's attention.

A Personal Story: Share a relevant anecdote that connects with your audience's experience and illustrates the problem you're going to address.

The B2B Sales Presentation

An Inspirational Quote: Incorporate a relevant quote that reflects the central message of your presentation and evokes an emotional impact.

A powerful start not only captures the audience's attention but also sets the tone and pace of your presentation, laying the groundwork for an engaging and inspiring delivery.

Chapter 5
Concise and Persuasive Body

Once you've captured your audience's attention with a compelling introduction, it's time to build the body of your presentation—the central part that develops your message and convinces your audience. This is where clarity, conciseness, and persuasion play a crucial role.

Develop your theme clearly and concisely, using specific examples and relevant data to support your arguments.

The body of your presentation should unfold your theme clearly and concisely, avoiding information overload and keeping the audience engaged at every step. To achieve this, it's essential to use clear and straightforward language, avoiding technical jargon and complex phrases.

Your audience seeks to understand your message and connect it with their needs. To make this easier, incorporate concrete

The B2B Sales Presentation

examples and relevant data that support your arguments. Statistics, success stories, and testimonials from satisfied customers can turn your ideas into tangible realities that resonate with your audience.

Imagine a presentation that merely lists benefits without offering evidence of their validity. Would it be convincing? Probably not. In contrast, a presentation that presents concrete data, success stories, and examples of how your product or service has solved real problems is much more persuasive and compelling.

The body of your presentation should weave together clear information, concrete examples, and solid arguments that convince your audience and compel them to take action

Chapter 6
Impactful Conclusion
Leaving a Lasting Impression on Your Audience's Mind

A memorable presentation doesn't end with your final point. The conclusion is your opportunity to leave a lasting impression on your audience, reinforcing your message and guiding them towards the desired action.

Leave a lasting impression with a closing that summarizes key points, presents a clear call to action, and sparks the need to move forward.

To create an impactful conclusion, it's crucial to succinctly and memorably summarize the key points of your presentation. Recap the key benefits of your product or service, remind them of the challenges your audience faces, and reaffirm how your solution can help them overcome these challenges.

The B2B Sales Presentation

Once you've reinforced your message, it's time to present a clear and compelling call to action. What do you want your audience to do after hearing your presentation? Do you want them to contact you for more information? Sign up for a demonstration? Make a purchase?

Craft a concise and clear call to action that indicates the next step and generates the urgency to move forward.

An impactful conclusion not only leaves a lasting impression on your audience's mind but also motivates them to take action. It's the endpoint of your journey that turns your presentation into a memorable and productive experience.

Chapter 7
Mastering the Stage
Tips for a Successful Presentation
Body Language and Non-Verbal Communication: Beyond Words

Your body language is a powerful communication tool that can convey confidence, enthusiasm, and credibility. A confident posture, direct eye contact, and expressive gestures can make the difference between a passive presentation and one that captivates the audience.

Posture: Maintain an upright and relaxed posture, avoiding stiffness or slouching. A confident posture conveys trust and assurance in your message.

Eye Contact: Establish eye contact with your audience, looking directly into their eyes. This creates a personal connection and conveys authenticity.

The B2B Sales Presentation

Gestures: Use natural and expressive gestures to emphasize your words and to maintain the audience's attention.

Effective Communication: Speaking with Passion and Enthusiasm

Speak with passion and enthusiasm about your topic. Your enthusiasm is contagious and can inspire your audience. Use clear and simple language that is easy to understand and connects with your audience's experience.

Clarity: Use clear and concise words to express your message. Avoid technical jargon and complex phrases.

Pacing: Vary the pace of your voice to maintain the audience's attention and to emphasize key points of your message.

Mastering the Tools: Using Visual Resources Effectively

The B2B Sales Presentation

Visual tools such as slides, graphics, and videos can significantly enhance your presentation, making it more engaging and informative. Use these tools effectively to illustrate your points and to keep the audience's attention.

Images and Graphics: Use high-quality images and relevant graphics that support your message. Avoid generic images and information overload.

Videos: Incorporate short and compelling videos that illustrate your message or showcase success stories.

Animations: Use animations to bring your slides to life and to maintain the audience's attention.

Mastering the stage is a combination of verbal and non-verbal communication, presentation skills, and deep knowledge of your topic. With practice and dedication, you can become a compelling speaker who captures attention and persuades your audience

Chapter 8
Effective Communication Speaking with Passion and Enthusiasm, Connecting with Your Audience

Words have power. They can inspire, persuade, inform, and move. In the realm of presentations, effective communication is key to connecting with your audience and conveying your message with clarity and conviction.

Speak with passion and enthusiasm, using clear and simple language that is easy to understand.

Your enthusiasm is contagious. When you speak passionately about your topic, your audience is impacted by your energy and credibility. Passion acts as a magnet that grabs attention and connects with the emotions of your audience.

The B2B Sales Presentation

Avoid technical jargon, complex phrases, and dull language. Speak naturally and fluently, as if you were conversing with a friend.

Effective communication blends passion, clarity, and simplicity. When you speak with enthusiasm, use accessible language, and connect with your audience on a personal level, your presentation becomes persuasive and engaging.

The B2B Sales Presentation

Chapter 9
Mastering Tools
Visual Resources that Capture Attention and Clarify the Message

In today's world, where attention is a scarce commodity, visual tools have become a crucial ally in capturing audience attention and conveying messages clearly and convincingly. Slides, graphics, and videos can transform an ordinary presentation into a dynamic and impactful experience.

Use Visual Resources like Slides, Graphics, and Videos to Illustrate Your Points and Maintain Audience Attention.

Slides are powerful instruments for presenting information in an organized and appealing manner. Utilize high-quality images, informative graphics, and clean, attractive design to complement your message and keep the audience engaged.

The B2B Sales Presentation

Graphics are ideal for visually presenting data in an easy-to-understand and visually appealing manner. Use bar charts, line graphs, pie charts, or maps to illustrate trends, comparisons, and relationships between data points.

Videos can breathe life into your presentation, adding a dynamic and engaging element. Incorporate short and concise videos to showcase success stories, product demonstrations, or animations that illustrate your message.

Avoid Information Overload and Excessive Text on Slides.

Remember that slides should complement your presentation, not replace it. Avoid information overload and excessive text on slides. Use a clean and attractive design that highlights the key points of your message.

Visual tools are powerful allies in capturing audience attention and conveying your message clearly and convincingly. Use these tools effectively and let images and

The B2B Sales Presentation

videos work to attract attention and keep your audience engaged.

What strategies have you found most effective in using visual aids to enhance your presentations? Understanding these dynamics can significantly impact how engaging and impactful your presentations become.

Chapter 10
Time Management
A Precious Resource That Must Be Respected

In B2B sales, time is a precious resource. Your audience has a full agenda and clear expectations regarding the duration of your presentation. Respecting the allocated time demonstrates consideration and professionalism, strengthening your image and building trust in your message.

Carefully Plan Your Presentation and Respect the Allocated Time. "Before stepping on stage," dedicate time to meticulously plan your presentation. Estimate how much time you will need for each section and ensure your content fits within the allocated time frame, avoiding unnecessary prolongation of the presentation.

Once your presentation begins, stay within the time limits you've set. Deviating from

The B2B Sales Presentation

the plan is likely to cause the audience to lose interest and feel frustrated.

Time is a valuable resource. Respecting your audience's time demonstrates professionalism and consideration, enhancing your image and helping you build strong relationships.

Chapter 11
Tips for Capturing Attention and Generating Interest Connecting Emotionally Through Stories and Examples

A successful presentation not only conveys information but also connects with the emotions of the audience, making it more memorable and persuasive. To achieve this, it is essential to use narrative tools that capture attention and generate interest.

Stories are a powerful instrument for connecting with the audience's emotions and making information more memorable. Stories allow us to tap into the human experience, build empathy, and create an emotional bond with the audience.

Use real-life stories that illustrate the benefits of your product or service or demonstrate how you have solved your clients' problems. Personal anecdotes or success stories can effectively engage your

The B2B Sales Presentation

audience and make your message more memorable.

Concrete examples are also valuable tools for capturing the audience's attention and making information more relevant. Use examples that are easy to understand and illustrate the key points of your message.

Stories and examples can transform a dry and technical presentation into a memorable and convincing experience. Use these narrative tools effectively to connect with your audience's emotions, making your message more powerful and persuasive.

Chapter 12
Incorporating Humor
A Touch of Lightness for a Memorable Presentation

In the context of B2B presentations, where seriousness and formality often prevail, a touch of humor can be a powerful ally to capture the audience's attention, relax the atmosphere, and make your message more memorable.

Appropriate Humor can make the presentation more engaging. A good joke or a funny anecdote can bring a smile to the audience and create a more personal connection. However, it's crucial to use humor carefully and responsibly, considering the context of the presentation and the type of audience you're addressing.

Humor should be suitable for the occasion, avoiding being offensive or derogatory. A well-placed joke can ease tension, make

The B2B Sales Presentation

information easier to digest, and create a more enjoyable atmosphere.

Examples of Appropriate Humor:

Self-deprecation: A bit of self-deprecating humor can break the ice and show that you don't take yourself too seriously.

Situational Humor: Use humor related to the industry or challenges your audience faces.

Analogies and Metaphors: Employ humorous analogies and metaphors to explain complex concepts more easily.

Tips for Incorporating Humor:

Be authentic: Let your humor reflect your genuine personality.

Don't overdo it: A little humor goes a long way. Avoid trying too hard to be a comedian.

The B2B Sales Presentation

Read your audience's reaction: If your humor isn't well-received, be flexible and adjust your approach.

Humor can be one of the tools to connect with your audience and make your presentation more memorable. Use humor thoughtfully and responsibly to turn your presentation into an enjoyable and persuasive experience.

Chapter 13
Create Interaction
Engage Your Audience and Foster Conversation

A presentation is not a monologue; it's a conversation. Engaging your audience is key to making your presentation more dynamic and memorable. Asking questions that invite audience participation fosters conversation and creates a more interactive environment.

Questions are a powerful tool to capture the audience's attention, assess their understanding, and stimulate discussion. Pose open-ended questions that encourage reflection and allow audience members to share their ideas and experiences.

Examples of Interactive Questions:

"What challenges are you currently facing in your industry?"

The B2B Sales Presentation

"What are your thoughts on the latest market trends?"
"What would you like to see in a product or service like the one I'm presenting?"
Tips for Asking Effective Questions:

Maintain a friendly and encouraging tone.
Avoid focusing on yes-or-no questions.
Pay attention to audience responses and use the information to further the conversation.
Questions are a powerful way to connect with your audience, demonstrate your interest in their opinions, and make your presentation more dynamic and participatory.

Epilogue

In this journey through the art of B2B sales presentation, we have explored strategies and techniques that will enable you to connect with your audience, capture their attention, persuade them, and become a true master of commercial communication. We have learned the importance of meticulous preparation, mastery in storytelling, mastery of body language, strategic use of visual aids, and creating a memorable experience that drives action.

Mastering the art of presentation is a continuous process of learning and refinement. Practice your technique, seek feedback from your audience, and do not be discouraged by challenges. With dedication and persistence, you can become a persuasive speaker who inspires confidence and turns their presentations into a driver of success for their business.

About the Author

Dionisio Melo is recognized throughout Latin America for his distinguished career in sales, where he has developed highly effective strategies for the region's demanding market.

His influence spans multiple dimensions: he is not only a prominent speaker and expert guide in sales training and coaching for salespeople, but also a prolific author on topics of sales, management, coaching, and leadership.

His books reflect his commitment to excellence and his ability to tackle specific challenges across various sectors.

Melo reaches a wide audience through newsletters and an influential blog shared on numerous business and sales specialized websites.

As a business advisor, Melo plays a crucial role in the success of companies in the

The B2B Sales Presentation

competitive Latin American market, offering tailored solutions that drive growth and competitiveness.

His presence at conferences and seminars ensures that his ideas and knowledge are accessible to sales professionals across the region, keeping them updated with the latest trends.

Dionisio Melo stands out not only for his personalized and effective strategies, but also for his comprehensive approach to sales team development, from motivation to problem-solving, consolidating his position as an influential and respected figure in Latin America.

www.ingramcontent.com/pod-product-compliance
Lightning Source LLC
Chambersburg PA
CBHW072055230526
45479CB00010B/1092